# DYSPHAGIA COOKBOOK

# FOR SENIORS

## Delicious and Nutritious Recipes for Seniors with Swallowing Difficulties

Dr. R ____ Brugger

# TABLE OF CONTENTS

# INTRODUCTION

A medical term for having trouble swallowing food and liquids is dysphagia. While this condition can affect people of any age, older adults are more likely to develop it. Numerous conditions, including Parkinson's disease, stroke, head trauma, neurological problems, and throat and mouth cancers, can result in dysphagia. Common dysphagia symptoms include choking or coughing while eating, feeling like food is stuck in the throat, trouble starting to swallow, regurgitation of food, and weight loss as a result of reduced food intake.

Dysphagia can have detrimental effects, including pneumonia, dehydration, malnutrition, and a decreased quality of life. Determining the root of dysphagia's occurrence is crucial for proper management.

Seniors with dysphagia frequently struggle to eat enough because they may have trouble swallowing food and liquids. Malnutrition may result from this, which could make their health situation even worse. Malnutrition in older adults can result in immune system impairment, muscle atrophy, and fatigue. Additionally, it can raise the chance of fractures, falls, and hospitalization.

Therefore, offering seniors with dysphagia nutrient-dense food options that are simple to swallow and digest is crucial. These foods ought to be nutrient-rich in order to help seniors maintain their immune system, muscle mass, and bone density. Nutrients like protein, vitamins, and minerals can also help.

**How This Cookbook May Be Useful**

Seniors and their caregivers who are looking for nourishing and delectable meal options that are simple to swallow will find The Dysphagia Cookbook for Seniors to be a valuable resource. This cookbook offers a huge selection of dishes that are especially created for seniors who have trouble swallowing.

While still flavorful and nutritious, these recipes use ingredients that are simple to chew and swallow.

The cookbook also offers helpful hints on how to prepare meals, such as how to adapt recipes to meet specific needs, how to use food thickeners, and how to make sure meals are aesthetically pleasing and appetizing. This cookbook's meal-type-based organization makes it simple to find the ideal recipe for any occasion.

Overall, the Dysphagia Cookbook for Seniors is a vital tool for anyone looking after a loved one who has trouble swallowing. This cookbook can enhance seniors' overall health and quality of life by offering them a variety of wholesome and delectable meal options.

# WHOLESOME MEALS RECIPES

## Creamy macaroni and cheese with softly cooked Broccoli

**Ingredients:.**

1 macaroni that has not been cooked.

1 cup of softly cooked broccoli.

butter, one tablespoon.

1 tablespoon flour.

a cup of milk.

1/2 cup of cheddar cheese, shredded.

To taste, add salt and pepper.

## Instructions:

Cook macaroni as directed on the package until very soft, then drain and set aside.

Chop broccoli into small pieces after steaming broccoli until very soft.

Melt butter in a tiny pot over low heat.

Cook for 1-2 minutes after smoothing out the flour with a whisk.

Add the milk gradually while whisking constantly to avoid lumps. Cook until the mixture becomes thick.

Add the cheese shavings and stir until it is smooth and melted.

Add the cooked macaroni and broccoli, stirring to combine.

Add pepper and salt to taste when seasoning.

Serve warm

# Rice noodles and Soft Tofu with vegetables

## Ingredients:

1 package of small-pieced soft tofu.

1 cup of softly cooked vegetables, like broccoli, bell peppers, and carrots.

1 tablespoon of oil.

1 tablespoon of soy sauce.

One tablespoon of honey.

1/2 teaspoon of garlic powder.

1/8 teaspoon of onion powder.

one-half of cooked rice noodles.

## Instructions:

Over medium heat, warm oil in a nonstick pan.

Add the tofu and cook it for a few minutes, until just lightly browned.

Stir in the cooked vegetables.

Soy sauce, honey, onion powder, garlic powder, add together in a small bowl.

As you pour the sauce over the tofu and vegetables in the pan, stir to evenly distribute it.

Stir the cooked rice noodles into the pan until they are thoroughly heated. Serve.

# Soft bread and pureed carrot and ginger soup

## Ingredients:

2 softly cooked carrots.

Softly cooked potatoes.

butter, one tablespoon.

1/2 cup of vegetable or chicken broth.

14 tsp. of ginger root.

To taste, add salt and pepper.

dipping bread that is soft.

## Instructions:

Cooked carrots and potatoes should be smoothed out in a blender or food processor.

Melt butter in a tiny pot over low heat. Vegetable purée is added; combine by stirring.

While whisking continuously to avoid lumps, gradually add the broth. Cook until thoroughly heated.

Stir in the ground ginger after adding it.

Add pepper and salt to taste. Warm up and serve with soft bread for dipping.

# Mashed potatoes, soft turkey meatballs, and cauliflower puree

## Ingredients:

cooked cauliflower (soft)

cooked potatoes (soft)

1 tablespoon of butter

Salt and pepper.

Soft turkey meatballs (see directions below).

## Ingredients for soft turkey meatballs

turkey meat that weighs half a pound.

one-fourth cup of breadcrumbs.

1 egg

1/4 teaspoon of salt

1/8 teaspoon black pepper

## Instructions:

Cooked potatoes and cauliflower should be thoroughly blended in a blender or food processor.

Butter should be melted slowly in a small pot. Stir in the pureed vegetables after adding them.

To taste, add salt and pepper to the food.

With tender turkey meatballs, serve warm.

## The following is for the soft turkey meatballs:

Set the oven to 375 degrees Fahrenheit.

Ground turkey, breadcrumbs, an egg that has been beaten, salt, and pepper are all combined in a bowl. Combine completely after mixing.

Form the mixture into tiny balls with a spoon or small cookie scoop, and then arrange the balls on a baking sheet covered with parchment paper.

Until thoroughly cooked, bake for 15-20 minutes. Serve warm alongside mashed potatoes and cauliflower puree.

# Pureed broccoli and cheddar soup with soft bread

## Ingredients:

Softly cooked broccoli.

one tablespoon of butter.

one tablespoon of flour.

1 cup of milk.

1/2 cup of cheddar cheese, shredded.

To taste, add salt and pepper.

Soft bread for dipping

## Instructions:

Cooked broccoli should be smoothed out in a blender or food processor.

Butter should be melted slowly in a small pot. Cook for 1-2 minutes after adding flour and whisking until smooth.

Whisk continuously to avoid lumps as you gradually add the milk. Cook until the mixture becomes thick.

When the cheese is melted and smooth, add the cheese shreds and stir.

Stir in the pureed broccoli before serving.

Add pepper and salt to taste when seasoning.

Serve warm with soft bread for dipping.

# Creamy mashed potatoes with cooked Carrots

## **Ingredients:**

Peeled and chopped two large potatoes.

Peeled and chopped two large carrots.

two tablespoons of unsalted butter.

1/4 cup whole milk.

Salt and pepper.

## Instructions:

The potatoes and carrots should be peeled and cut into small pieces.

For 20 minutes or until they are tender, boil the potatoes and carrots in a pot of water.

Add the butter, milk, salt, and pepper to the pot after draining the water.

Use a fork or a potato masher to mash the potatoes and carrots until they are creamy and smooth.

Serve the softly cooked carrots alongside the creamy mashed potatoes.

# Pureed butternut squash with soft dinner roll

## Ingredients:

Peeled and cubed one medium-sized butternut squash

1 tablespoon of unsalted butter

1/4 cup whole milk

As desired, add salt and pepper

One soft dinner roll

## Instructions:

The butternut squash should be peeled and cut into small pieces.

For 20 minutes, or until it is soft, boil the butternut squash in a pot of water.

After draining the water from the pot, add the butter, milk, salt, and pepper.

In a blender or food processor, puree the butternut squash until it is smooth.

Serve a soft dinner roll alongside the butternut squash puree.

# Creamy tomato soup with soft crackers

## Ingredients:

Tomato soup in a can

1/4 cup whole milk

Salt and pepper

Crackers

## Instructions:

The tomato soup should be heated in a pot over medium heat.

Stir well after adding the milk, salt, and pepper to the pot.

The tomato soup should be heated all the way through after 10 minutes of simmering.

Serve soft crackers alongside the creamy tomato soup.

## Cooked oatmeal with mashed banana and honey

**Ingredients:**

One cup of quick-cooking oats

one cup of water

1/4 cup of whole milk.

1 mashed banana

1 teaspoon of honey

**Instructions:**

Quick-cooking oats and water are combined in a pot and heated to a boil over medium-high heat.

While stirring occasionally, lower the heat to a simmering level and cook the oatmeal for 5-7 minutes.

Mix well after adding the milk, honey, and mashed banana to the pot.

Oatmeal should be simmered for a further five minutes, or until it is soft and creamy.

With mashed bananas and honey, serve the soft cooked oatmeal.

# Rice Pudding with mashed Berries

**Ingredients:**

one cup of cooked rice

1 glass of whole milk

1/3 cup of sugar

1/8 teaspoon of cinnamon powder

1/4 teaspoon of ground nutmeg

Mash 1/4 cup of berries

**Instructions:**

In a pot, mix the cooked rice with the milk, sugar, cinnamon, and nutmeg. Heat to a boil.

Rice pudding will simmer for 20 to 25 minutes while being stirred now and then on low heat.

Stir vigorously after adding the mashed berries to the pot.

Once the rice pudding is soft and creamy, simmer it for an additional 5 to 10 minutes.

Combined with mashed berries, serve the soft cooked rice pudding.

# SMOOTHIE RECIPES

## Strawberry banana smoothie

### Ingredients:

1 banana, sliced

1 cup frozen strawberries

1 cup of Greek yogurt

1/2 cup milk (use a thicker milk such as whole milk for easier swallowing)

1 teaspoon honey (optional)

### Instructions:

Add all the ingredients in a blender.

Blend until smooth. If necessary, add more milk to achieve the desired consistency.

# Banana Almond Milk Smoothie

## Ingredients:

1 banana, sliced

1 cup almond milk (use a thicker consistency like vanilla almond milk for easier swallowing)

1/2 cup Greek yogurt

1 teaspoon honey (optional)

## Instructions:

Add all ingredients in a blender. Blend until smooth.

If desired, add more almond milk to desired consistency.

# Avocado Spinach Smoothie

## Ingredients:

1/2 ripe avocado, pitted and peeled

1 cup spinach leaves

1/2 cup Greek yogurt

1/2 cup milk (use a thicker milk such as whole milk for easier swallowing)

Juice of 1/2 lime (optional)

## Instructions:

Add all the ingredients in a blender.

Blend until smooth. If necessary, add more milk to achieve the desired consistency.

# Cherry and almond milk smoothie

## Ingredients:

1 cup frozen cherries

1 cup almond milk (use a thicker consistency such as vanilla-flavored almond milk for easier swallowing)

1/2 cup Greek yogurt

1 teaspoon honey (optional)

## Instructions:

Add all ingredients in a blender. Blend until smooth.

If desired, add more almond milk to desired consistency.

# Kale and pineapple smoothie

## Ingredients:

1 cup cabbage leaves

1 cup frozen pineapple

1/2 cup Greek yogurt

1/2 cup milk (use a thicker milk like whole milk for easier swallowing)

1 teaspoon honey (optional)

## Instructions:

Add all ingredients in a blender. Blend until smooth. If necessary, add more milk to achieve the desired consistency.

**Note:** For smoother smoothies, you can strain them through a fine mesh sieve to remove larger pieces of fruit or vegetables. This step is optional and may depend on a person's individual swallowing ability.

# 28-DAYS MEAL PLAN

## Week 1:

### Day 1:

**Breakfast:** Soft cooked oatmeal with mashed bananas and honey

**Lunch:** Pureed carrot and ginger soup with soft bread

**Dinner:** Creamy mashed potatoes with soft cooked carrots

### Day 2:

**Breakfast:** Soft cooked rice pudding with mashed berries

**Lunch:** Soft tofu and vegetable stir-fry with rice noodles

**Dinner:** Pureed cauliflower with mashed potatoes and soft turkey meatballs

**Day 3:**
**Breakfast:** Soft cooked oatmeal with mashed bananas and honey
**Lunch:** Pureed butternut squash with soft dinner roll
**Dinner:** Creamy macaroni and cheese with soft cooked broccoli

**Day 4:**
**Breakfast:** Soft cooked rice pudding with mashed berries
**Lunch:** Pureed broccoli and cheddar soup with soft bread
**Dinner:** Soft tofu and vegetable stir-fry with rice noodles

**Day 5:**

**Breakfast:** Soft cooked oatmeal with mashed bananas and honey

**Lunch:** Creamy mashed potatoes with soft cooked carrots

**Dinner:** Pureed cauliflower with mashed potatoes and soft turkey meatballs

**Day 6:**

**Breakfast:** Soft cooked rice pudding with mashed berries

**Lunch:** Creamy tomato soup with soft crackers

**Dinner:** Creamy macaroni and cheese with soft cooked broccoli

**Day 7:**

**Breakfast:** Soft cooked oatmeal with mashed bananas and honey

**Lunch:** Pureed butternut squash with soft dinner roll

**Dinner:** Pureed broccoli and cheddar soup with soft bread

## Week 2:

**Day 8:**

**Breakfast:** Soft cooked rice pudding with mashed berries

**Lunch:** Soft tofu and vegetable stir-fry with rice noodles

**Dinner:** Creamy mashed potatoes with soft cooked carrots

**Day 9:**

**Breakfast:** Soft cooked oatmeal with mashed bananas and honey

**Lunch:** Pureed cauliflower with mashed potatoes and soft turkey meatballs

**Dinner:** Creamy macaroni and cheese with soft cooked broccoli

**Day 10:**

**Breakfast:** Soft cooked rice pudding with mashed berries

**Lunch:** Pureed butternut squash with soft dinner roll

**Dinner:** Pureed broccoli and cheddar soup with soft bread

**Day 11:**

**Breakfast:** Soft cooked oatmeal with mashed bananas and honey

**Lunch:** Creamy tomato soup with soft crackers

**Dinner:** Soft tofu and vegetable stir-fry with rice noodles

**Day 12:**

**Breakfast:** Soft cooked rice pudding with mashed berries

**Lunch:** Pureed carrot and ginger soup with soft bread

**Dinner:** Pureed cauliflower with mashed potatoes and soft turkey meatballs

**Day 13:**

**Breakfast:** Soft cooked oatmeal with mashed bananas and honey

**Lunch:** Creamy mashed potatoes with soft cooked carrots

**Dinner:** Creamy macaroni and cheese with soft cooked broccoli

**Day 14:**

**Breakfast:** Soft cooked rice pudding with mashed berries

**Lunch:** Pureed butternut squash with soft dinner roll

**Dinner:** Pureed broccoli and cheddar soup with soft bread

## Week 3:

**Day 15:**

**Breakfast:** Soft cooked oatmeal with mashed bananas and honey

**Lunch:** Soft tofu and vegetable stir-fry with rice noodles

**Dinner:** Creamy mashed potatoes with soft cooked carrots

**Day 16:**

**Breakfast:** Soft cooked rice pudding with mashed berries

**Lunch:** Pureed cauliflower with mashed potatoes and soft turkey meatballs

**Dinner:** Creamy macaroni and cheese with soft cooked broccoli

**Day 17:**

**Breakfast:** Soft cooked oatmeal with mashed bananas and honey

**Lunch:** Pureed butternut squash with soft dinner roll

**Dinner:** Pureed broccoli and cheddar soup

**Day 18:**

**Breakfast:** Soft cooked rice pudding with mashed berries

**Lunch:** Creamy tomato soup with soft crackers

**Dinner:** Soft tofu and vegetable stir-fry with rice noodles

**Smoothie:** Strawberry and banana smoothie

**Day 19:**

**Breakfast:** Soft cooked oatmeal with mashed bananas and honey

**Lunch:** Pureed cauliflower with mashed potatoes and soft turkey meatballs

**Dinner:** Creamy macaroni and cheese with soft cooked broccoli

**Smoothie:** Kale and pineapple smoothie

**Day 20:**

**Breakfast:** Soft cooked rice pudding with mashed berries

**Lunch:** Pureed butternut squash with soft dinner roll

**Dinner:** Pureed broccoli and cheddar soup with soft bread

**Smoothie:** Banana and almond milk smoothie

**Day 21:**

**Breakfast:** Soft cooked oatmeal with mashed bananas and honey

**Lunch:** Creamy mashed potatoes with soft cooked carrots

**Dinner:** Soft tofu and vegetable stir-fry with rice noodles

**Smoothie:** Avocado and spinach smoothie

## Week 4:

**Day 22:**

**Breakfast:** Soft cooked rice pudding with mashed berries

**Lunch:** Pureed cauliflower with mashed potatoes and soft turkey meatballs

**Dinner:** Creamy macaroni and cheese with soft cooked broccoli

**Smoothie:** Cherry and almond milk smoothie

**Day 23:**

**Breakfast:** Soft cooked oatmeal with mashed bananas and honey

**Lunch:** Pureed butternut squash with soft dinner roll

**Dinner:** Pureed broccoli and cheddar soup with soft bread

**Smoothie:** Strawberry and banana smoothie

**Day 24:**

**Breakfast:** Soft cooked rice pudding with mashed berries

**Lunch:** Soft tofu and vegetable stir-fry with rice noodles

**Dinner:** Creamy mashed potatoes with soft cooked carrots

**Smoothie:** Kale and pineapple smoothie

**Day 25:**

**Breakfast:** Soft cooked oatmeal with mashed bananas and honey

**Lunch:** Pureed cauliflower with mashed potatoes and soft turkey meatballs

**Dinner:** Creamy macaroni and cheese with soft cooked broccoli

**Smoothie:** Avocado and spinach smoothie

**Day 26:**

**Breakfast:** Soft cooked rice pudding with mashed berries

**Lunch:** Pureed butternut squash with soft dinner roll

**Dinner:** Pureed broccoli and cheddar soup with soft bread

**Smoothie:** Cherry and almond milk smoothie

**Day 27:**

**Breakfast:** Soft cooked oatmeal with mashed bananas and honey

**Lunch:** Soft tofu and vegetable stir-fry with rice noodles

**Dinner:** Creamy mashed potatoes with soft cooked carrots

**Smoothie:** Strawberry and banana smoothie

**Day 28:**

**Breakfast:** Soft cooked rice pudding with mashed berries

**Lunch:** Pureed cauliflower with mashed potatoes and soft turkey meatballs

**Dinner:** Creamy macaroni and cheese with soft cooked broccoli

**Smoothie:** Kale and pineapple smoothie

**Note:** It's important to consult a medical professional before making any dietary changes, especially for seniors with dysphagia. This meal plan is only a suggestion and can be adjusted according to individual dietary requirements and restrictions.

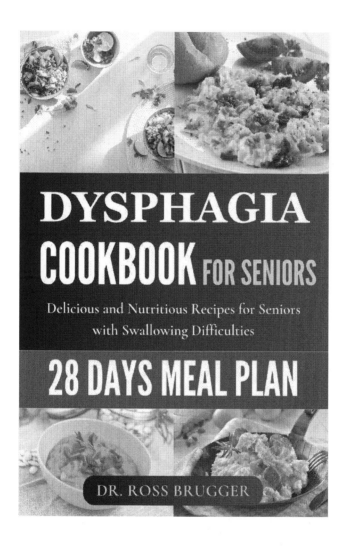

DYSPHAGIA
COOKBOOK FOR SENIORS

Delicious and Nutritious Recipes for Seniors
with Swallowing Difficulties

28 DAYS MEAL PLAN

DR. ROSS BRUGGER

Made in the USA
Middletown, DE
26 July 2023

35770192R00033